TAKE A
CLOSER
LOOK

Volume Two: Fifty More

Copyright

TAKE A CLOSER LOOK; *Learn to See Through Manipulations, Distortions and Fabrications*, Volume 2 by David Allan Van Nostrand.

© 2018 David Allan Van Nostrand

All right reserved. No portion of this book may be reproduced in any form without written permission of the author.

ISBN: 9781791995782

TABLE OF CONTENTS

Introduction 1
Gatekeepers 3
The Brand App Experience 5
Nuts 7
Ford's Aha! Moment 9
I Think We Can All Agree, Don't You? 11
Shop 'til Somebody Drops 13
McBummer 15
How Your Company's Research is Like Drug Trials 17
Your Shower Is Leaking 19
A Little Bird Told Me 21
How to Lead a Group to Make Bad Decisions 23
Who Let the Dogs In? 25
How to Gain 11 Pounds 27
Where Are Your Ancestors From? 30
Show Me the Money 32
The Sky Is Falling! 34
My Smart TV Is Doing What? 36
You Say Potato 38
The Other Wheel of Fortune 40
An Automotive Brand Loyalty Surprise 42
How to Be as Successful as Buffett, Gates, and Cuban Without the Effort
 45
Online Reviews: Fact or Fiction? 47
A.I. vs H.I. 49
Can I Buy You a Drink? 51
Let's Use the Internet to Vote on Our New Flag 53
The Nina, The Pinta and the Mayochup 55
McCadillac 57
Nipper Favored His Master's Voice 59
Insert Tab A into Slot B 61
The Glamour of International Business Travel 64
Second Prize Is a Set of Steak Knives 68
How the TED Talks Became the Ted Baxter Talks 70
Which of the Seven Dwarfs is the Tallest? 72
Put on Your Thinking Caps 74

Cool	76
Butch Cassidy, the Sundance Kid, and Beer	78
7 Things You Don't Know About Wireless-only People	81
TIDAL Wave	84
The Swiss Army and Their Knife	86
Big Data, Artificial Intelligence, and Cockroaches	88
Deities, Ghosts, and Aliens from Other Planets	90
Order, Please	92
Which Is It?	94
Musical Chairs	96
Pay Only for What You Keep	98
Violent Destructive Windstorms	100
Marriage Causes Divorce	102
The Other Levi-Strauss	104
Mixed Emotions	106
Dear Diary	108
It's Time to Eat	110
Another One Bites the Dust	112
About the Author	114

Introduction

This book can be enlightening, entertaining, and sometimes amusing.

It can also be one of the most important books some people ever read.

If you are one of the strivers and achievers who fully grasp and internalize the issues and concepts in this book, you will know more about how to tell good information from bad than The Boss does.

My first book was a collection of 50 lessons I taught in Graduate Business School, written for anyone who uses information, which is most of us.

I continued to write weekly articles after I stopped teaching, with less of an eye to business *students* and more of an eye to business *professionals*.

As it is the executive decision-makers who are making mistakes seen so often, this book is an enormously valuable tool for XDM2Bs (executive-decision-makers-to-be).

The lessons are practical ones, and most topics are taken from the news.

They take only a few minutes to read.

Their convenient snack-size makes them ideally suited to be read in short bursts, so take this book with you. You will be able to read an article or two whenever you are waiting in an office or in traffic.

They are purposely not organized by theme.

Open the book at random and take pot luck, or choose a title that catches your eye from the table of contents.

Want to stand out at work? Give a copy of this book to The Boss. Want to lay low? Don't.

These articles are about facts and foibles, truths and lies – you know, stuff in the news and in every presentation and report you've ever seen.

The undercurrent of each of these 50 articles is that <u>most of the information executive decision-makers see is manipulated, distorted, and fabricated – and they are completely unaware of it because gatekeepers censor it</u>.

Gatekeepers

Hundreds of years ago, a *gatekeeper* was the person whose only job was to prevent people from entering a restricted area without permission.

In the modern workplace, gatekeepers not only control *access* (to decision-makers), but also *information*. The control of information is double trouble as it works in both directions - up <u>and</u> down the ladder.

Information gatekeepers are everywhere in hierarchical organizations. There are usually several layers of them, and their power is often greater than their formally recognized authority.

Gatekeepers control agendas and distort outcomes.

They are rarely good stewards who carefully and responsibly manage that which has been entrusted to their care. When information comes across their desks, most gatekeepers change it before passing it along, particularly in ways that make themselves look good.

Gatekeepers alter information by making choices that are a complex web of motive, bias, prejudice, and worse. <u>Gatekeepers abuse their power by acting in their own self-interests</u>, unilaterally deciding what to discard and what to change before passing it up and down the ladder.

What happens to a company's research more often than not is a deliberate *stacking of the deck* by one or more gatekeepers. This English-language idiom is defined as *influencing the results in an unfair manner by surreptitiously pre-arranging things to achieve a desired outcome.*

When it comes to reporting research findings in hierarchical organizations, most of the original information is withheld and what remains is elaborately embroidered.

The more gatekeepers there are between the research and the The Boss, the more manipulations, distortions, and fabrications get delivered to The Boss' desk.

Gatekeepers are only one of the *Misinformation Traps* that keep The Boss from getting the whole picture, warts and all.

How many of the others do you know about?

The Brand App Experience

There are more than five million mobile apps, yet consumers download only a tiny fraction of them and regularly use no more than a dozen or so.

Mobile users favor them over websites and expect them to be fast, comprehensive, and easy to use.

How big is the brand app market?

According to Forrester Analytics, U.S. shoppers are expected to make $118 billion in retail purchases through their smartphones in 2018, up from $13 billion only five years earlier.

Deloitte says "Brands view apps as a golden opportunity to communicate directly with consumers and in a more meaningful, long term manner. When brands get it right, the returns can be huge."

Getting it right means the apps are built with the user's needs in mind. Users want brand apps to:

- Have a real functionality.
- Provide features that are genuinely meaningful.
- Solve a problem.

But most are getting it wrong.

An online survey of 1,000 brand app users by WillowTree generated these key findings:

- Users say only half of brand apps turn out to be useful; the majority do not address their needs.

- Half of users say the branded app experience is such a poor one that they delete the app after just one use.
- Negative brand app experiences lead people to make fewer purchases.

The even bigger problem is how most consumers avoid brand apps because they see them as just a one-way marketing tool, and not as anything meaningful to them.

The best-rated mobile brand apps?

We don't think many will be surprised that Nordstrom, Starbucks, Walmart, and Amazon have the most well-liked mobile apps.

What do outsider evaluations have to say about your company's mobile apps?

Nuts

William Black opened a store in New York City in 1926 where he sold roasted nuts.

As the story goes, he called it Chock Full o' Nuts because the tiny (6 by 20 foot) store was crammed full of dozens of types of nuts.

Within six years, he had more than 100 nut shops in the city. Then along came the Great Depression. Nuts became a too-expensive luxury item, so he converted his stores to small coffee shops, brewing his own blend, and the changeover was a successful one.

The coffee was popular with New Yorkers, and in 1953, Black began selling his Chock Full o' Nuts coffee in grocery stores. It quickly became New York's best-selling coffee.

In the sixties, Black's wife, a cabaret vocalist, began singing the "Heavenly Coffee" jingle in the company's televised advertisements and on sponsored broadcasts.

The reason I bring this up is a recent NY Times article I read. In it, writer James Barron said they recently added a "No Nuts" disclaimer on their coffee can – *in response to people thinking the coffee includes some kind of nuts.*

Well, no kidding.

Dennis Crawford, senior marketing manager, said, "Every time we've done consumer research on why people do not purchase the product, the number one thing that comes back to us is *there's something in the coffee.*"

Well, no kidding.

Chock Full o' Nuts discovered this "number one thing" long ago and have ignored it ever since, which means people will continue to think *there's something in the coffee* for a long time to come. The name telegraphs quite clearly that this product is FULL OF NUTS.

Executives say the confusion is for those who live outside New York. Which leaves out 300 million people in the U.S. alone. But who cares about them?

Ford's Aha! Moment

In an interview with Wall Street Journal business columnist John Stoll, Jim Farley, Ford's president of global markets, says he is going to turn the advertising world on its head.

Farley said Ford will laser-target us with very specific ads online, using algorithms that mine social media and online searches.

He shook people up when he said two things are true, both of which have them cringing in the halls over at WPP, who has the Ford account now.

One is that development and placement of digital ads can be done better by machines and software than by people. The other is that *the new ad work will not be given to the big traditional agencies.*

Late in the interview, this came up:

Farley told WSJ he had one of the most fascinating days of his career when his leadership team rode around in vehicles with actual customers.

"They don't know how our navigation system works, they have three phones attached to the dashboard, they're driving with their knees," he said, adding that when they saw real people in real life, "It was a huge 'aha' moment for us."

Gee whiz, Jim. Seeing real people in real life is an 'aha' moment for the head of a $44 billion company?

The cornerstone of good research is learning from actual people in actual situations.

Farley said this 'aha' moment convinced him Ford needs deeper thought into how customers actually use products. "It's just the process of being curious about the right things and getting out of Detroit."

It's not just getting out of Detroit, Jim.

What is far more important is *getting away from marketers* whose interest is in *influencing* people, and spending more time with researchers whose interest is in *understanding* people.

It's also getting away from engineers who focus on *things*, and spending more time with researchers who are interested in understanding *how people use things*.

When you - the head of the company - don't know about such crucially important issues for consumers, there are two common explanations.

One is that your research people are as hidebound as your ad agencies and should be up for review, too. The other is that your research is good, but gatekeepers are keeping it from you.

Either way, you are unaware of what's going on.

I Think We Can All Agree, Don't You?

Most of us know *groupthink* is the situation where people in meetings are pressured to agree with the stance championed by the most senior executive.

We know it occurs when consensus is considered more valuable than asking questions or challenging the status quo.

The insidious part is how groupthink absolutely guarantees people will accept conclusions they believe are incorrect or invalid and thus <u>learn to avoid thinking critically</u> - about any issue, situation, or decision.

We have seen leaders who say they have eliminated groupthink by making fact-based decisions.

What most of them fail to recognize is their facts aren't really facts at all. They are assumptions that go unchallenged by employees who know it is dangerous to disagree.

Too many business leaders are manipulated by provider companies whose primary goal is pleasing their clients.

The best way for the less ethical ones to do this is by learning what executives hope to find and then providing exactly that. Harvard Business Review says too many leaders shoot themselves in the foot by revealing their personal biases up front.

There are hundreds of advisors who provide paint-by-number lists of what leaders can do to overcome groupthink.

A particular favorite is when they tell leaders to *encourage their staffs to speak openly*. This sounds to us like when your mother said it's okay to say you don't like the gift she gave you and would prefer something else. Yeah, sure - ask anyone who tried it.

So what <u>does</u> work, you ask?

- Start by realizing groupthink is a constant danger and actively make plans to deal with it.

- Don't just encourage people to speak their minds – insist on it – and reward them when they do.

- Break up large teams into smaller teams. If you still get groupthink, you'll at least get different versions.

- Never state your opinions first. Follow the policy of the U.S. military, where staffs are required to state their opinions in reverse order of rank, saving the boss' comments for last.

And for braver souls?

Be different – actively seek people who will tell you something you need to know, won't like to hear, and others won't tell you.

If you have the courage, that is.

Shop 'til Somebody Drops

Thousands of years ago, all humans were hunters of wild animals and gatherers of wild foods.

Responsibilities were designated by gender.

Men were bigger and stronger, so hunting became a male task. Women, already rearing the children, took the responsibility for gathering readily-available edibles such as fruits, nuts, and berries.

Hunters needed to find the game first.

As they roamed farther and farther from the camp, they learned how to track game animals and read signs. Over time, they developed the specialized skills of locating their prey, and of equal importance, <u>finding their way back home.</u>

Gatherers needed to know how to tell edibles from poisons and how to select fruits, nuts, and berries that were ripe and thereby more flavorful and more easily digestible.

Psychologists say our tens of thousands of years of practicing these skills still manifest themselves today in the ways we shop.

Men are on a mission; women are on a journey of discovery.

Men go in and out of stores more quickly. They go directly to what they want and quit when they have captured it. Women shop in a more leisurely fashion. They take a more selective approach, using their greater sensitivity to assess subtle differences.

Studies show that on average, men get bored after half an hour of shopping, while women don't get bored for two hours or more. Little wonder how when they shop together, *women feel hurried and men feel it takes forever.*

Thousands of years of hunting developed spatial awareness and navigational skills, too.

Studies have shown that men tend to navigate by creating mental maps of a territory and then imagining their position on the maps. Women are more likely to remember their routes using landmarks.

So when someone says men's greater ability to navigate is hooey, tell them male and female *navigational skills were honed differently by evolution for different tasks.*

McBummer

We came upon a story in Fortune that said McDonald's partnership with UberEats is bringing in younger customers. We looked around some more and found a CNBC article that said McDonald's is losing customers and a Global Data report that said McDonald's has seen an increase in customers 50 and older.

Wait a minute.

More younger customers + more older customers = fewer customers?

Curious as to how this could be, we called Neil Saunders, Managing Director at GlobalData, producers of more than 15,000 research reports a year. He explained several things to us about what their restaurant research is showing.

He said the new younger customers are typically in their late teens and early twenties, with lower incomes. Because they don't own cars, they rely on delivery, mostly late at night and mostly pizzas. But now that McDonald's delivers, they have become new customers switching to an entirely new menu experience.

Older customers, he said, are coming more often in the morning for McCafé coffee and bakery items. They are also drawn in by the new interior design, with its neutral tones, softer lighting and more and better seating options.

So who is leaving?

Saunders says the loss is among GenXers and Millennials. This is a bad sign for McDonald's, as these age groups have long been their sweet spot. Saunders told us these prime customers are leaving McDonald's for deal-related promotions and for regional and niche restaurants.

We asked him about yet another article, this time in Forbes, that said McDonald's is losing market share in breakfast and the need to fix it is urgent. He told us it's true because GlobalData sees former customers increasingly going to competitors like Dunkin' Donuts, Burger King and Taco Bell.

When franchisees are asked about their relationships with McDonald's executives, the average grade is a D-.

A big source of frustration for franchise operators is how the much-ballyhooed All-Day Breakfast is not bringing in new customers like it was supposed to. Worse yet, sales of burgers and fries are being cannibalized by existing customers who are ordering cheaper breakfast items instead.

As if that weren't enough, having to make breakfast all day adds cost, complexity and congestion, a sore spot for franchisees who feel executives are out of touch.

Chief Executive Steve Easterbrook, in a McDonald's press release, said "We're executing the right strategy to achieve long-term, profitable growth."

How Your Company's Research is Like Drug Trials

Those who provide the money for research want to hear good news, so it is not surprising that many researchers are willing to see they get it. How?

One way is by interpreting findings in a positive light. We see this in particular when the goal of a study is *validation*.

Validation **is defined as the action of** *proving, confirming, justifying, and endorsing.*

Validation is starting with the answer and ensuring the research supports what is already assumed to be the best course of action. <u>It is not objectively testing to determine if it really is</u>. If you direct someone to conduct a validation study, they will do just that.

Another way to guarantee positive results is to select samples that are positively inclined towards the company and/or the product.

One company we worked with had previously done all its new product research with the same group of diehard loyalists who always produced rave reviews for the new product-to-be. <u>This egregious failure of sampling was completely unknown to the senior executives.</u>

A proven way to influence research outcomes is to suppress negative findings.

An independent study published in the New England Journal of Medicine showed 97% of positive clinical trials (those that found the drug was effective) were published.

When studies found the drug was not effective, only 8% were published.

In business, when the research report contains bad news, it is rarely seen by executives.

In most companies, *marketing gatekeepers* show only the research that supports the story they want to tell, and <u>anything that doesn't support that position is left on the cutting room floor</u>.

Executives are unlikely to ever see their company's research.

Instead, they are shown a few doctored slides included in a flashy marketing presentation.

It is our position that validation is for parking lot receipts.

Your Shower Is Leaking

The condo board told a friend her shower was leaking into the apartments below. She was ordered to under no circumstances use the shower until it was repaired.

Faced with an undiagnosed amount of serious plumbing work, she began by going to the home improvement store to pick out some new tiles.

That was not the place to start.

Before the plumbing could be repaired, the entire structure had to be demolished. This took several days, producing hundreds of pounds of concrete and ceramic rubble that had to be carried away.

Once the surrounding structure was removed, workers had to remove every bit of the old plumbing and replace everything with new materials. This also took several days.

As replacement often leads to upgrade, she ended up buying new fixtures and all the little things that make them work. The workers installed all this, taking yet more days.

Only after all the structural work was completed could the tiling begin.

This, too, took days.

With a brand-new shower, the rest of the bathroom seemed shabby, so she had the entire bathroom redone. Several weeks later, the end result looked great.

She had begun the shower project the very same way most companies begin research projects.

Most research, especially when led by non-experts, focuses on the appearance of the end product, and not upon the crucial underpinnings that must be dealt with first in the appropriate sequence.

Good research begins with answering two simple, yet critical questions.

- What do we want to know?
- How do want to be able to use the information?

Please note that good research does not begin with a fancy presentation deck where the story has already been written and awaits only some cherry-picked data to fill in the blanks.

Note also that when we start at the right place – first things first – information goals and research objectives are likely to evolve beyond the initially oversimplified definition, *which means what we learn has more and greater value.*

Where does your company's research begin?

A Little Bird Told Me

An excellent article by Steve Lohr in the NY Times tells us *False News Spreads Faster and Wider, and Humans Are to Blame*.

He cites a study by Sinan Aral from MIT's Sloan School of Management that analyzed ten years of Twitter stories spread by three million people.

Aral's team used information from six independent fact-checking organizations to establish if the stories were true or false. Then they counted retweets. They found that not only were lies 70% more likely to be re-tweeted, but also that lies travel faster and farther.

Our tendency to retweet lies has significant consequences now that nearly two-thirds of Americans get at least some of their news via social media portals and feeds.

So why do people share false stories?

False claims are more eye-catching. Aral says this is no surprise, as falsehoods are made up to be whatever the writer wants and honest information isn't.

Another reason is that people rarely read the entire message they pass on. Our *cognitive biases* are triggered when we are presented with the right kind of algorithmically selected meme.

And of course when we desire to be among the first to "know," we willingly sacrifice accuracy for speed.

Taking "news" at face value is typical.

Stopping to determine the true sources of stories and the motivations behind them is hard mental work. It takes a lot effort, is more deliberate, and requires intellectual discipline.

As with so many other things, it's your choice to make.

You can be one of the herd that get their *likelier-to-be-lies news* from social media, or you can be one of the few who make the decision to trust only reliable sources.

Most don't know how to determine a source's reliability. Do you?

How to Lead a Group to Make Bad Decisions

Begin by ignoring the principles of good decision-making and problem-solving. This is easiest if you don't bother to learn what they are in the first place.

Announce at the beginning of every meeting the course of action you've already decided upon. This way, your group needn't bother themselves with anything other than rubber-stamping your decisions.

Make it clear that you are not interested in anyone questioning anything and that disagreement and pushback have no place in your organization. Use words like "loyalty" and "commitment" to get across the message that you value conformity above all else.

Limit discussion to a few carefully chosen courses of action. If alternatives are presented, ignore the ones you don't like.

Make absolutely certain you:

- Ensure your group sees the world through a biased, narrow lens. Don't seek external opinions, because *outsiders are troublemakers.*

- Choose only information that supports your position and ignore or discredit the rest. The "data-approved mantle of legitimacy" will convince your group they've made the right decisions.

- Rush to premature conclusions. Waste no time identifying and examining alternatives. Value hurrying to endorse pre-defined "answers" rather than wasting time asking questions.

- Remind your employees of the Japanese proverb about *the nail that sticks out gets hammered down.*

Groupthink.

This is defined as a pattern of thought characterized by self-deception and forced manufacture of conformity.

When we pressure groups to agree, we are guaranteeing they will fail to think critically about issues, situations, and decisions.

Groupthink occurs when the desire for consensus overrides the commitment to present alternatives, critique positions, and express unpopular opinions. In a groupthink situation, individuals refrain from doubting or disagreeing with the artificially manufactured consensus. Groupthink leads to carelessness and irrational thinking because it values conformity above all else.

You will still have one problem, though.

Your best people will see through this and either complain outside your meetings or look for work elsewhere.

Today's big question: How many people who need to read this do you have the courage to forward it to?

Who Let the Dogs In?

More than half of dog owners share their beds with their dogs, about the same number who regard dogs as members of their families.

Size matters.

According the American Pet Products Association, 32% of large dogs sleep with their owners, compared to 41% of medium-sized dogs, and 62% of small dogs.

A new study.

In a recent study by the Center for Sleep Medicine at the Mayo Clinic, both dogs and humans wore activity monitors that recorded the soundness of their sleep.

The study concluded that a dog's presence in the bedroom may not be disruptive to human sleep, as was previously suspected, but the dog's position on or off the bed did make a difference.

Pros and cons.

Time says sleeping with your dog is good for you, but admits the Mayo study included only 40 people, most of whom were healthy, middle-aged women. We'd like to point out that the study did not control for the size or temperament of the dog or the human.

In another survey, this one of 23,000 dog owners, more than half of the owners reported that their dog bedmates woke them at least once a night.

After looking at the findings from these studies, the Daily News says having your dog sleep in the bedroom is fine, but having it in the bed with you is not.

Why do so many do it?

The American Kennel Club says aboriginal Australians slept with their dogs for warmth (hence the name of the band, Three Dog Night) and for protection from evil spirits.

Barkpost.com is in favor of sleeping with dogs, saying they help us relax, they make us feel safe, and it makes the dogs happy. They also point out dogs in bed can disturb our sleep, aggravate allergies, come between us and our partners, and may lead to aggressive behavior – presumably that of the dog.

What none of these sources mentioned was that some people whose sleep has been disrupted by dogs have kicked them out of bed.

On the bed or off, the dogs always slept better than the owners.

How to Gain 11 Pounds

USA Today says 90% of Americans don't like to cook. A Harris poll says 80% do. Harvard Business Review says 10% love to cook and 45% hate it.

Why the disparity?

Some is due to samples and methods, and some is due to using terms that are closely related but not the same. Liking is not loving and disliking is not hating. The biggest reason for these inconsistencies, though, is our definitions of what actually constitute cooking.

So what do we mean by "cooking?"

In addition to the heating method (baking, frying, grilling, etc), "cooking" has for a very long time meant the entire process of everything that comes after shopping and before eating: washing, trimming, chopping, measuring, stirring, etc.

Ask anyone who runs a restaurant, and they'll tell you most of the labor of cooking is in the preparation activities that begin early every morning and go on all day long.

Today, people who microwave frozen dinners, heat cans of soup, or make sandwiches say they are cooking.

Eating at home doesn't mean cooking, either.

Among meals eaten at home, few of them involve even the remotest definition of cooking. More of them than ever before are takeout, home delivery, and prepared meals bought at the grocery. According to Consumer Reports, prepared meals are a $29 billion-a-year business, growing twice as fast as overall grocery store sales.

Cooking has become a spectator sport.

As Americans cook less, they watch people cooking on television more. A Harris poll says eight out of ten adults watch cooking shows. The Telegraph says UK residents spend more time watching cooking shows than they do actually cooking.

The doyenne of television cooking, Julia Child, was not interested in making cooking fast or easy. For her, it was a matter of deep personal enjoyment.

Today's cooking shows are less about the pleasure of cooking and more about selling stuff.

These shows encourage home cooks to take all manner of shortcuts, each of which involves buying another product. *More than four in ten* viewers have bought kitchen gadgets or appliances as a direct result of something they saw on a cooking show.

People who watch cooking shows on television gain more weight.

According to a Cornell University study, of the 14 ways cooking habits are influenced (magazines, blogs, YouTube, etc), watching cooking shows was the only one associated with significant weight gain.

The Washington Post says what is mainly learned from television is not cooking at all, but *culinary fashion*, which takes the form of cooks preparing rich foods with high butter and fat contents. The study's author, Lizzy Pope, said "Because many cooking shows normalize overconsumption and gratification, it comes as no surprise that viewers' culinary habits are negatively influenced."

Negatively influenced, indeed.

Those who cook using recipes from television weigh 11 pounds more than those who don't.

Bon appétit.

Where Are Your Ancestors From?

It depends.

Phil Rogers, a Chicago news reporter, recently sent samples from home test kits to several computerized DNA sequencing services.

One told him his ancestors were from Ireland and Scotland. Another said Portugal. Others said Scandinavia, Peru, and Afghanistan.

How can this be?

There are three components of computing:

- *Data* is information that has been turned into numbers.
- *Databases* are collections of data organized for rapid search and retrieval.
- *Algorithms* are formulas devised by persons for solving problems.

Each company Rogers mailed his DNA to used different information, different data sets, and different formulas. And of course each claimed to be superior to the others.

When information, databases, and algorithms vary, results vary.

UCLA geneticist Dr Wayne Grody says there might be some vague truths somewhere, but home DNA test kits are mostly like the quack cure-alls pitched by snake oil salesmen a hundred years ago.

The culprit.

Artificial Intelligence isn't artificial at all, but an unfortunately chosen term used to describe *machine learning*.

Most people think A.I. is something new, even though it's been around since 1956, when scientists began to develop "thinking machines." Encyclopedia Britannica says A.I. is "the ability of a computer to carry out tasks commonly associated with intelligent beings." Think of it as the ability to recognize patterns and perform calculations within huge data sets at blindingly fast speeds.

But as many have demonstrated, A.I.'s information and databases vary greatly, and algorithms ignore context, which leads to many completely meaningless conclusions.

Woof.

The reporter submitted DNA from his Labrador Retriever to the same services.

One company did not notice the sample was non-human, and concluded in their report that this person would be great at basketball.

Show Me the Money

United Airlines announced last week it would stop giving bonuses to its employees.

Individual bonuses would be replaced by a lottery that would give a few big prizes to a few lucky winners. According to United, the lottery would increase motivation, build excitement, and provide workers with a sense of accomplishment.

Employees felt they were being played for suckers.

They said it was clear to them United's real motivation was to cut costs. A closer look at the old and new programs revealed that dumping traditional bonuses in favor of a sweepstakes would save United tens of millions of dollars a year.

It might have worked as a part of an above-and-beyond reward system, but not as a replacement for traditional compensation.

Who thought this was a good idea?

To be effective, incentives need to be defined as *meaningful and attainable* by the recipients, not by the executives.

Under the new system, 98% of United's employees would get nothing. How's that for meaningful and attainable?

Deb Gabor, a brand strategy consultant, said "When a company creates compensation programs without obvious ties to the company's strategic objectives, it creates friction against the company's brand. United created a system that rewards randomness rather than consistency."

United's reaction to the unexpected backlash was to say they are "pressing the pause button."

Scott Kirby, United's president, said "Our intention was to introduce a better, more exciting program, but we misjudged how these changes would be received." Forbes says the idea was doomed from the start.

A United spokesperson said – with an apparent lack of irony – "Right now we are going to collect feedback from our employees to make sure we create a new incentive program that will be meaningful to employees."

Wouldn't collecting feedback from employees have been the smart place to start?

Negative *unintended consequences* invariably occur when out-of-touch decision-makers press "solutions" and "rewards" on people who don't define them as such.

How do your customers and employees view the things you consider to be meaningful and attainable?

The Sky Is Falling!

In an excellent article in the NY Times: *Lies, Damned Lies, and One Very Misleading Statistic*, Amanda Taub takes a closer look at a sexual misconduct scandal reported in The Sun, a British tabloid. Their headline shrieked that "a bombshell report" had found "UN aid workers raped 60,000 people in Haiti."

Taub decided to take a closer look at the sources of these statistics and concluded *the 60,000 number was horrifying, attention-grabbing, and <u>completely made-up</u>*.

Where did the 60,000 come from?

A 2017 United Nations report said it had recorded 311 victims of sexual misconduct by peacekeepers in Haiti the previous year. Note this was for *all types of sexual misconduct, not just rape*. The mislabeling is more sensational, isn't it?

Andrew McLeod, a former UN employee, wrote a two-page memo about that report and used it to solicit support for a new nonprofit he was founding.

In his report, he assumed there were other groups behaving as badly, and doubled the actual 311 to a rounded 600. This is a <u>guess</u>, not a statistic.

Then he assumed that only 10% of incidents get reported, and so bumped his number to 6,000. This is <u>speculation</u>, not a statistic.

The original number was for one year (2016) and not big enough, so the report writer concluded the ten-year total was 60,000, a far-fetched assumption.

Guessing, speculating, and assuming are *anti-factual*.

Big numbers make the point more powerfully than small.

It is in storytellers' interests to exaggerate, especially when they are seeking financial support. This type of manipulation, distortion, and fabrication is far more common than most think.

The more we hear something, the more we believe it.

As this story was reported and re-reported without question by many channels and outlets, each repetition served to reinforce our assumption that it must be true, because we heard it so often.

The basic psychological concept at work here is called the *illusory truth effect*. Our very human tendency is to believe information that is repeated. *And the more it is repeated, the more we believe it.* And the more it is repeated, the more we believe it. See?

Emily Dreyfuss calls the illusory truth effect "a glitch in the human psyche that equates repetition with truth." No one knows this better than marketers and politicians.

Sarah Martin, consultant to the UN on gender-based violence, said this kind of false statistics "discredit the very brave women and children who came forward."

This irresponsibly sensational series of assumptions turned a 331-person fact into a 60,000-person fiction.

(Today's title is taken from the tale of the hysterical Chicken Little, who mistakes a falling acorn for the end of the world.)

My Smart TV Is Doing What?

Since the earliest days of television, Nielsen has ruled the TV audience-measuring roost. Using a combination of set meters, code readers, and personal diaries, they have collected Americans' viewing habits and sold the data to networks and advertisers since 1950.

But they're in trouble now.

By the end of this year, three-fourths of all households in the U.S. will have smart TVs with *Samba* pre-installed.

Samba has paid all the major television manufacturers to install their software, which suggests shows based on what you've been watching, just like Netflix. They make their money by selling the detailed tracking data they have on more than 13 million viewers.

Their tracking is real-time, so advertisers get it immediately, instead of waiting for Nielsen reports. It is more accurate, too.

Samba has the additional ability to recognize and identify <u>all your devices</u> that use the same internet connection as your TV.

This goes far beyond viewing habits.

Samba tracks you wherever you go and uses your TV watching data to send ads to your phones, tablets, and laptops.

It is unlikely these were the kinds of "special offers" you had in mind when you agreed to opt in.

Executives say more than 90% of users of smart TVs opted in, but for what? David Kitchen, a London software engineer, said "You appear to opt into a discovery-recommendation service, but what you're really opting into is *pervasive monitoring*."

On their website, Samba makes no bones about where the real value lies, promising advertisers they can "Discover what TV audiences are watching and activate data- and device- synching across screens to amplify media investments."

Most of us are unaware of when our information is compromised, which happens more and more often. As a matter of fact, we read about it so often that most of us don't even notice anymore.

You Say Potato

In my early days as a researcher, I had proudly produced what I believed to be an excellent piece of research only to be told – after the fact, of course – that it wasn't what sponsors were looking for. Although they never said it outright, it was easy to see their dissatisfaction was a result of *hoping for a fairy tale with a happy ending and getting the facts of life instead.*

I had failed to get all involved to agree on the definitions of what we were looking for before we started, and I vowed it wouldn't happen again.

Years later, along came an assignment where the client was interested the attitudes and behaviors of a highly targeted elderly population.

Like many words, "elderly" is defined in many ways. Before we began, we needed to ensure that the entire team agreed upon a shared definition of "elderly."

The most obvious way to define elderly is by age, of course.

This isn't as simple as it seems. Our investigation came across definitions of 55, 60, 62, 65, and 70 in published studies. These differences made age-based data comparisons from one study to the next quite useless.

Another way of looking at age is through the eyes of the beholder. To a child, 18 is old. To a teenager, 40 is ancient. To a 60-year old, 80 is elderly.

Dictionaries say elderly is defined as "characteristic of later life" and "showing signs of age." Less attractive synonyms include "over the hill" and "on one's last legs."

So what are some of the things that are characteristic of later life?

The process of aging is a biological reality that occurs at different rates for different people. Some in their 70s are highly active; others in their 50s are well into decline. Many people with excellent vision are surprised to find they need reading glasses when they are in their early 40s.

It's not as if we step though a doorway as fully-functioning adults and come out the other side as blithering idiots.

For most, it is more like slowly going down a very long slope. As our skills *gradually decrease*, our feelings of disorientation, frustration, and anxiety increase. And these emotions lead to feelings of *vulnerability*, which is defined as "needing special care, support, or protection because of age or disability."

We ended up evolving a more holistic definition.

We included chronological age, but were more focused on gradually-diminishing physical, sensory, and cognitive skills *and needs for special care.*

The lessons.

Never assume we all share the same definitions. We should go beyond the superficial and when the need arises, develop our own deeper, more meaningful definitions.

The Other Wheel of Fortune

The NY Times' Daniel Slotnik wrote a great obituary about a bewildered-looking man in a rumpled suit who won millions of dollars playing roulette. The man claimed to have used a computer program to create a winning system.

He lied.

What he did was observe very, very carefully over a long period of time and detect patterns that were *invisible to others*.

He knew that while all roulette wheels looked the same, each was minutely different. The slight variations that occurred during manufacture, assembly, and installation went unnoticed by most.

Richard Jarecki had an unnaturally keen eye for detail.

Like every other player, he knew that the odds were with the casinos. As there were 37 possible numbers and the payout was 35:1, the edge would go to every casino with perfectly manufactured and perfectly balanced wheels.

But the wheels were not perfectly manufactured or balanced, and the imperfections were there to be discovered by a very patient and very observing person. Once Jarecki learned the idiosyncrasies of a particular wheel, the odds were in his favor and he would win big.

Casinos notice when people win more than they should, and take steps to counter them.

We have all seen this in movies where a gambler beats the house, typically by counting cards at blackjack tables.

Casinos knew Jarecki knew something, so they would move the wheels around to try and throw him off. But unbeknownst to them, he had paid such attention to detail that he could tell which wheel was which by tiny nicks and scratches that most of us would never notice.

This is the same difference that we find between highly perceptive researchers and all the rest.

Patience and undivided attention reveal things that most don't notice. And when you know something the others don't, you've got a real edge over the house.

An Automotive Brand Loyalty Surprise

Priceonomics writes stories about data provided by their customers. Their website says they are "obsessed with creating and spreading quality, data-driven information." Their latest story is titled *Which Car Brands Have the Most Loyal Owners?*

When we took a closer look, we found all is not what it appears to be, for several reasons.

- First, casual readers conclude the story is about new cars, but the study included only used cars. This leaves out the 17 million new car buyers each year in the U.S.
- Second, findings include only CarMax shoppers. CarMax sells a million used cars a year, which is only about 2% of the 43 million used cars sold in the US. each year.
- Third, their findings are only for people who traded in one used car on another.

Which car brands have the most loyal owners?

It depends on which study you read.

According to the hugely slanted CarMax study, **Lexus**, Mercedes-Benz and Ford are the top three auto brands for customer loyalty. Others study car brand loyalty, too, so we looked at some research from other sources and saw none found the same results.

Here are the top three auto brands for customer loyalty as reported by six other auto information sources:

- *BrandKeys*: **Hyundai**, Ford, and Toyota.
- *Experian*: **Ram**, Ford F150, Lincoln.
- *Edmunds*: **Toyota**, Subaru and Honda.
- *Cartelligent*: **BMW**, Lexus, Audi.
- *Consumer Reports*: **Ford**, Toyota, Chevrolet.
- *Autoguide*: **Land Rover**, Mercedes-Benz, Lincoln.

There you have it.

Seven different studies identify 14 different auto brands in the top three and seven different brands in first place.

Researchers are seldom surprised to see such differences in findings from analyses that claim they are studying the same thing. Studies that appear in the media rarely include descriptions of methods, samples, or how terms are defined. Further, studies cited in news stories almost never include multiple data sources.

Loyalty.

Real loyalty is consistently purchasing the same brand over an extended period of time. True auto loyalty would be buying the same brand three, four, five times in a row and more, wouldn't it? And wouldn't loyalty be more important with new cars than used?

So what we have from Priceonomics is a measurement that if accurately titled would say: *A One-Shot Analysis of Brand Repurchase Among People Trading in One Used Car for Another at a CarMax Dealership*. This is miles away from their title.

Neither Priceonomics nor CarMax has any interest in telling you about study limitations.

What about the studies your company uses to make important decisions? Do you know their limitations?

We'd bet not.

How to Be as Successful as Buffett, Gates, and Cuban Without the Effort

Warren Buffett spends 80% of his day reading, Mark Cuban reads three hours a day, and Bill Gates reads a book a week.

Most successful people agree that reading books is important because *it is a difficult mental task that requires focus and guides deeper thinking.*

Inc. says business leaders believe that deep reading cultivates in them the knowledge, habits, and skills needed to make decisions, plan, and prioritize.

So to be more like successful people, we need to adopt their reading habits, right?

Not according to Blinklist, who says there is no need for us to waste all those hours reading books when we can read summaries in only 15 minutes.

Blinklist is one of many companies that sell book summaries for busy people on the go. They are the modern equivalent of Cliffs Notes, who started the whole book summary business in 1958. Less-dedicated university students who had been assigned books to read wouldn't bother, reading only the short outlines instead. Millions of Cliffs Notes were sold to <u>students who were satisfied to go through college the cheap and easy way</u>.

Sensitive to these criticisms, Cliffs Notes said their outlines were never intended to replace reading the full books and "Students who use them in this way are denying themselves the very education that they are presumably giving their most vital years to achieve." Wink, wink, nudge, nudge.

Let's take this save-time-reading-books premise a step further.

Why should we waste minutes on a book when we can "read" it in seconds?

- *Outliers*. Hard work and talent are great, but the secret is luck.
- *Lean In*. Women can overcome obstacles by speaking up.
- *The Black Swan*. People are very good at fooling themselves.

So who is more attracted to summaries than real books?

Mostly people who don't want to interrupt their entertainment with reading. The latest reports tell us that Americans spend eight to ten hours a day using smartphones and watching television.

No wonder they read so few books.

Online Reviews: Fact or Fiction?

Most of us read about the Virginia restaurant that refused to serve a White House staffer and within 24 hours found ten thousand negative reviews had been posted on Yelp.

Yelp's reaction was to say the restaurant's rating had been affected by reactions to news coverage rather than reviewers' personal experiences. Trip Advisor temporarily froze their online reviews when the same thing happened to them.

There are many terms used to describe the posting of deliberately false reviews for personal reasons (*brigading, sock puppeting, astroturfing, etc*). But what is more important than the lingo is how the rate of incidence is rapidly increasing. And what do you think is at the center of the phenomenon?

Artificial Intelligence.

Business Insider reports that mathematicians have taught A.I. to write believable fake reviews that sneak past screening algorithms in an escalating cycle of one-upmanship.

Think of it as like the software hacking/patching cycle, where we constantly need to update our apps.

It is the equivalent of an arms race where each new offense is countered by a new defense that is overcome by a new offense, and so on. And just like an arms race, the speed, magnitude, and coordination of these activities are growing, too.

Studies show between 80% and 90% of us use online ratings in our decision-making.

Yelp's estimates say that fake reviews make up 25% of all reviews. Amazon says 40% are fakes, and the Washington Post says it's 50%. The Telegraph summarizes it neatly: "Given the clandestine nature of the fake reviews, it would almost impossible to arrive at a credible figure."

Studies show 85% of us are unable to tell fake reviews from real ones.

Not a problem, many say, as there is plenty of advice available to help us sort the fakes from the true ones.

They are absolutely right.

We can find scads of information on the InterWeb that tells us how to recognize fake information (shorter comments, smaller words, no details). But wiser heads know that *the people behind fake reviews read this advice too, and revise their algorithms accordingly.*

The idea that we can easily see through sophisticated efforts to produce fake reviews is sheer nonsense.

It might be a good idea to put less trust in online ratings and more in the Human Intelligence approach of asking friends and co-workers about their experiences, processing the data, and making up your own mind.

A.I. vs H.I.

An article in Gizmodo says scientists have developed a way to identify people by their walk.

They did this in the highly controlled environment of a lab where they filmed study subjects walking on a special pressure-sensitive floor. An A.I. system analyzed weight distribution, pace, and three-dimensional measures of 120 study subjects.

Omar Reyes, the lead author, said "Distinguishing between the subtle variations from person to person is extremely difficult to define manually, which is why we had to come up with a novel A.I. system to solve this challenge from a new perspective."

Which got us to thinking about those subtle variations and how real people distinguish them now.

Walking is defined as moving along by putting one foot in front of the other, allowing each to touch the ground before lifting the next.

Walking varies by style, speed, and intent.

Here are 20 types of walking; you will know even more:

Toddling is moving with short unsteady steps, and is how we all start.

Ambling, sauntering and *moseying* have to do with wandering about at a slow, easy pace. When we *sashay*, we glide nonchalantly. *Strolling* is also slow, but the purpose is for pleasure. *Meandering* has the same pace, too, but here we take an intentionally indirect course. *Rambling* is just wandering around with no particular destination in mind, and when we *traipse*, we walk aimlessly without finding or reaching our goals.

When we walk without lifting our feet, we *shuffle*. *Trudging* is walking wearily with a lot of effort.

Tramping is walking with a firm, heavy, resounding step. *Stomping* is intentional, to show we are annoyed.

To *stride* is to walk with long steps – vigorously, hastily, or impatiently. When we're nervous, we *pace*.

Promenading is walking with the intention of showing off. When we *strut*, we are vain and pompous and our gait is self-affected. *Swaggering* is the top of this heap – a self-important, domineering, ostentatious display of arrogance and conceit.

Deep meaning usually involves nuance.

For the time being, it takes the human eye and the human brain and H.I. (Human Intelligence) to be able to distinguish the subtle variations of attitude and intent.

Tiptoeing is walking quietly on your toes so as not to disturb someone. *Slinking* is moving stealthily or furtively (as in fear or shame).

Can I Buy You a Drink?

The National Institutes of Health have shut down a controversial study of how moderate drinking promotes good health after a task force found severe ethical and scientific lapses in the study's planning and execution.

Credibility for sale.

The NY Times reported that officials of the National Institute on Alcohol Abuse and Alcoholism solicited $67 million from leaders of the U.S.'s $350 billion wine, beer and spirits industry by "strongly suggesting the study's results would endorse moderate drinking as healthy."

This ethical lapse was compounded by officials deliberately designing the study to minimize the likelihood of finding any problems.

The Washington Post said the study was inescapably compromised. Reuters said the study's funding undermined the integrity of the research process.

Dr. Michael Siegel, of Boston University's School of Public Health, said the study "is not public health research – it's marketing."

Does this ring any bells?

Historians will recall the very same thing happening in the tobacco industry. When it was becoming apparent that smoking was a severe health risk, tobacco companies adopted a five-point strategy:

- Fund research that supports the sponsor's position.
- Design research to find in favor of the sponsor's position.

- Hide findings that don't support the sponsor's position.
- Distort findings to maximize the sponsor's position.
- Deliver the sponsor's version of what the data say directly to decision-makers.

What about the gatekeepers in charge of so much corporate research, where there are no watchdogs, transparency advocates, referees, or nosy reporters?

Go ahead – guess.

In business, as in science and government, gatekeepers and study sponsors manipulate study designs to guarantee favored outcomes.

Research studies stack the deck by asking leading questions of *deliberately skewed samples* so the "answers" come out the way sponsors want them to. And when findings don't support the sponsors' positions, gatekeepers distort some and hide the rest.

Gatekeepers in business, science and government are adept at using supposedly scientific inquiry to *sell pre-determined outcomes to their bosses instead of the honest facts.*

Let's Use the Internet to Vote on Our New Flag

Estonia is in northern Europe, just south of Finland and just west of Russia. It was part of the USSR until 1991, when it declared its independence.

Sten Hankewitz, writing in Estonian World, tells us that when several small districts in the Kanepi region recently merged into one, it was decided they needed a new official coat of arms and flag.

The region's name comes from *kanep*, the Estonian word for hemp, which has been grown there for hundreds of years. *Hemp* is the form of cannabis that is used for industrial purposes, mostly cloth, rope, and oil. It is not the psychoactive form of cannabis that we know as marijuana.

To choose their new image, the council held a special contest.

In a preliminary round, 23 different works of art were submitted for consideration. Officials picked seven finalists and put them up for a vote. One was an icon featuring a cannabis leaf. According to the council, records show Kanepi farmers have used the cannabis leaf as their growers' co-op symbol for 150 years.

Modern times being what they are, the council conducted the vote online.

Of the 15,000 who voted, more than 12,000 chose the cannabis symbol. The council chairman said the process "was very democratic," in spite of the fact there are only 5,000 residents in the region.

According to Reuters, the council submitted the winning logo to Estonia's heraldry commission, where it was granted national approval.

Harry Anslinger, the notorious demonizer of marijuana in the 1930s, must be rolling in his grave.

The Nina, The Pinta and the Mayochup

In spite of what they taught us in school, Columbus did not discover America.

You might say he was the first European to arrive in the western hemisphere, but evidence suggests the Vikings got there 500 years before him. And never mind the Asians who 15,000 years ago came across the land bridge that connected Siberia and Alaska.

Enough of that history nonsense, you say. How about something important, like condiments?

Nearly a million people recently found the time to vote for their right to buy a pre-made blend called Mayochup.

The people at Heinz, masters of manipulation, allowed Twitter followers to "discover" mayonnaise and ketchup mixed together in the same bottle, <u>a triumphant solution in search of a non-existent problem.</u>

It is tarted up to pretend it is a new discovery, but there is nothing new about it.

Heinz already sells *Mayochup* in the Middle East. You can buy *Marie Rose Sauce* in Ireland and *Mayo-Ketchup* in the U.S. Other terms for mayonnaise-ketchup blends are *salsa rosado* and *fry sauce*.

PR flacks are saying things like "its arrival is going to be absolutely glorious," and "it's the perfect addition to almost any food." Time magazine says Heinz' New Mayochup has incited "total condiment mayhem."

Others are less breathless.

USA Today asks, "Is it a disgusting new condiment or just what you've been waiting for?" Fast Company asks "Is it innovation gone wrong?"

Jeff Vrabel called it a "cute viral Twitter poll run by stunt-inventing millennials in the employ of an enormous corporation."

Bethany Jean Clement is hotter under the collar than most. She says "This deeply stupid non-development represents not just the triumph of convenience over sense-making, but that of end-stage capitalism over human dignity. Combining the contents of two containers is now officially too much cooking for America, and the solution, of course, is to buy another thing."

For those who can't wait, Mayochup is available online at Kuwait's Sultan Centre and Dubai's Margin Fresh.

McCadillac

Let me see if I have this straight: Cadillac struggled to sell cars, so their solution was to leave Detroit for New York, where they struggled to sell cars, so their solution was to leave New York for Detroit. Really?

Four years ago, Cadillac hired aging hipster Johan de Nysschen to lead a brand transformation. Road & Track said "his expensive advertising campaigns showing emaciated, scraggly-bearded, tight-jacketed metrosexuals posed in rain-drenched back alleys urging the viewer to Dare Greatly, flopped miserably."

Four years later, de Nysschen is gone, but not before hiring Deborah Wahl, who claimed to have transformed McDonald's during her tenure there as Chief Marketing Officer.

Did she really?

Bizjournals says Wahl was pushed out because she didn't get the job done.

McDonald's president Steve Easterbrook said chasing customers who just won't go to a McDonald's was a mistake. And that was exactly who CMO Deborah Wahl was chasing when she said McDonald's needed to create ads that capitalize on "how teens and twenty-somethings are discovering information they trust."

How did that work out?

Wahl and her handpicked team of hundreds of millennial social media experts delivered messages, alright. The problem was <u>they weren't deemed believable or relevant</u>. Whoops!

So Cadillac's relo didn't work out, their president didn't work out, and now someone who couldn't sell $5 hamburgers is in charge of selling $50,000 cars?

We can hardly wait for the new ads.

Nipper Favored His Master's Voice

In 1899, when offered the famous *His Master's Voice* painting at sale, the Edison Bell Company rejected it, saying "dogs don't listen to phonographs."

Dogs incarcerated at the pound are not having the same soothing experience as those spending the day being pampered at the doggie spa.

Kennelled dogs are exposed to many stressors when locked up in strange, noisy, and bewildering environments. The experience is even worse for those who have been mistreated or are ill.

Treating shelter dogs well is the right thing to do.

It has a practical element, too. Well-adjusted dogs behave better, which makes them easier to place in adoptions and less likely to be returned.

The Scottish SPCA and the University of Glasgow conducted a study with kennelled dogs to learn ways to reduce the animals' stress. They collected physical and behavioral data and compared the results, noting that not all dogs react in the same ways and showing how stress levels vary by age, size, breed, and gonadal status.

Their study showed that classical, reggae, soft rock, Motown, and pop have measurable calming effects while heavy metal causes stress. No mention was made of bagpipe music or Kenny G.

The study also showed that *varying the music has a positive effect over time,* which suggests a playlist that includes Hound Dog, Walking the Dog, Hey Bulldog, and The Boxer.

In a surprise to many, listening to audiobooks had a more calming effect than listening to music.

Special psychoacoustically-designed music sold online was found to have no positive effects of any kind. This should cause consternation among those who pay $5 a month for doggy streaming services such as relaxmydog.com, who claim their specially formulated videos are watched more than 10 million times a month on YouTube.

For some, the soothing nature of relaxing audio isn't enough.

This is why we now have on-trend companies selling <u>doggy relaxation videos</u>. No word yet about the increase in stress brought about by your dogs fighting over the remote control and arguing about whether to watch Benji, Lassie, or 101 Dalmatians.

(Music historians know that Hound Dog, popularized by Elvis Presley, was first recorded by Big Mama Thornton.)

Insert Tab A into Slot B

Americans are famous for ignoring instruction manuals and plowing right in. Men are worse about it than women, and the younger we are, the less we bother with instructions or advice.

There are many reasons for this, but the biggest ones are that instruction manuals are too long, too dense, and too technical.

Of course they are, because of who writes them – tech experts – the worst possible choice for writing guides. They know the product inside and out and assume most of what they know needs no explanation. They also use scientific jargon the rest of us don't understand.

An unforgettable User Experience (UX) in the lab.

The engineers who had designed the product we were testing had been invited to observe from behind the mirrored glass.

As they watched an intelligent adult woman struggle with an absolutely awful set of instructions, they mocked her and called her stupid. They were, of course, shooting the messenger who was holding their poor design up to the light.

I told them she is not stupid – she is your customer, and there are millions just like her who will struggle with the same things she did. For this impertinence, I lost the account to someone who would agree that the fault is the customer's, not theirs. Good riddance.

Global products need to produce manuals in dozens of languages.

This leads to the inevitable translation and syntax errors we've all seen. There are so many of them that an entire wing in the YouTube Hall of Shame is devoted to embarrassing translation errors.

Using only pictures solves the language problems, like IKEA does with their instructions, but not everyone is a fan of crude black and white line drawings. Sure, picture-only directions avoid the need for translation and reduce printing costs, but they lose a lot, too.

The quality of the manual is closely related to the quality of the product.

Wiser consumers know this. They recognize that when a company doesn't care about making a quality product, they aren't likely to care about producing well-written setup and operating instructions.

Those in the know have learned the quality of the manual is an indicator of product quality and so they "comparison shop" product manuals before buying. They understand the best manuals are brief, simple, and to the point.

Really smart shoppers avoid products whose manuals are too dense, too mechanical, and have long FAQ sections. They agree with Mark Svenvold, author of *The Disappearance of the Instruction Manual*, who says the FAQ universe is filled with "answers to almost every question but the one you are asking."

What is the best way to write instruction manuals?

I don't know the best way, but here is how we do it:

- We start with outsiders from all walks of life.
- We give products to regular people without instructions or advice of any kind.

- We ask our study subjects to figure out how to put things together, turn them on, and use them.

Independently and with teams, paid volunteers work through things aloud.

They make mistakes, identify barriers and choke points, try different things, and arrive at solutions. Scientists collect and analyze the learnings and give them to people with real writing talent. Then we test them, again with regular people.

How do exceptional Executive Decision-Makers do it?

They take the responsibility for seeing that their instruction manuals are great because they:

- Begin by understanding how real people set up and use the product,
- Use what investigators learn to explain things simply, in print and on video so everyone can be happy, and
- Write not only a great manual, but a great Quick Start Guide, too.

The challenge is to explain procedures simply and directly, but without condescending - kind of like how we should be treating customers in general.

The Glamour of International Business Travel

After a long day of flying and hours of the weary traveler's shuffle-stop-shuffle-stop through immigration, baggage, and customs, I arrived at the airport rental car line as hot and tired as the dozen or so people already waiting in line ahead of me.

There were sixteen stations but only two clerks.

After standing in line for more than an hour to move forward 20 feet, I finally got to the counter and handed over my printouts. The clerk asked for my Colombian passport. What? I'm not a Colombian, I said, I'm an American, and I showed him my U.S. passport.

He insisted I didn't qualify for the special Colombian rate, and accused me of trying to game the system.

What special rate? What system?

Angrily, I asked for the manager, who gave me the same bad treatment. Neither one apologized, neither one suggested any alternative, and neither one offered to rent me a car under different terms. Boiling over, I called the agent an asshole, stormed out, and caught a cab to my hotel.

The next morning I went online and rented a Hyundai Elantra for a week from one of Enterprise's off-airport locations. When I went to pick it up, they didn't have an Elantra (or similar, as they say). Instead, they put me in an Accent, which is a much smaller car. An hour later, I brought it back and said it was too small for me and may I please have something larger? They gave me a Hyundai SUV and said there would be no extra charge.

Later that day I got a call from Budget's Joshua Yount.

He had seen the email I had sent to Budget's corporate customer service address and wanted to do four things:

- Apologize,
- Thoroughly and swiftly investigate the incident,
- Listen carefully as I told him all I remembered about my experience, and
- Make things right.

The very next day, Mr Yount called again, this time to tell me he had determined that Budget's algorithms had erroneously redirected my online reservation from the U.S. site to the Colombia site. He had also determined I could not have possibly known this.

Profoundly sorry for the error and the entire miserable incident, he reimbursed me for the cab rides I never should have needed and told me when I got my Enterprise bill, to please send it to him and he would reimburse me for that, too.

The Enterprise bill.

The receipt Enterprise sent me after I returned their car didn't look right, so I emailed them asking for an explanation. A day later, with no response, I emailed them again. Again, no response, so I tried a link to a different customer service address. It bounced back UNDELIVERABLE.

I called their customer service line and asked why Enterprise would put me in a smaller car when they didn't have the one I reserved, instead of upgrading me. And why they charged me $60 for the upgrade – after the fact. The phone rep said the company policy is to move customers up one car class when they don't have the car they reserved, at no extra charge. But here's the kicker – the individual sites don't have to follow company policy. Huh?

As to the upcharge, I learned that's also up to the individual sites. And my first two emails that were never answered? Their corporate algorithms had sent my emails directly to the rental location.

Let's see if I've got this straight – individual sites can, at their discretion, move me down a grade, upcharge me for something they shouldn't, and ignore my emails?

Everyone makes mistakes.

The important difference is in how they are handled.

Enterprise had a chance to convert me after Budget blundered badly, but the combination of their mishandling a simple request for billing information and Budget's desire to make things right drove me right back to Budget, where the whole thing started.

An interesting story, you say, but what's in it for me?

Nine out of ten people who have a bad experience with a company don't report it, typically because they don't want to waste the time and effort, no one will listen, and nothing will be done about it.

But they can't do anything about your problem if you don't tell them about your problem, and here's how I do it.

Calling is easier, but I like having a written record of the ongoing conversation so there are no misunderstandings later. I rough out my story as if I was telling it to a friend, edit it until I'm satisfied, and paste it into an email.

I send my story to email addresses I find online, writing to a manager when I can and cc'ing at least several executives.

Now I have given imperfect companies (and aren't they all?) a chance to show me what they're made of. Given a fair chance, some do the right thing.

Second Prize Is a Set of Steak Knives

A study of 1,500 salespeople who were promoted to managerial roles found outstanding sales performance predicted managerial failure more often than not.

Why?

Because the skills that made them successful salespeople were not the skills they needed to become successful managers.

Jay Fitzgerald of the National Bureau of Economic Research says the research is a confirmation of Laurence J. Peter's *Peter Principle,* the idea that employees in organizations will ultimately rise to their *level of incompetence.*

When executives make promotion decisions based upon employees' performance in their current roles, they are ignoring the importance of the skills that will be important in the new roles.

Leading a sales team takes a very different set of skills.

A key observable trait that can help predict which salespeople will make better managers is whether they have experience working within sales teams, rather than individually. The researchers found that employees with collaboration experience typically produce better results as managers.

Most executives also overlook the obvious - when they promote their best sales rep, *they lose the revenue of their best sales rep.*

The cream rises until it sours.

The Peter Principle doesn't apply only to sales, of course. People who excel at any position in an organization are often rewarded with higher positions, *eventually arriving at those that exceed their abilities.*

Dr Peter said every bureaucracy was inevitably made up almost entirely of people inadequate to their tasks. "In every organization," he said, "there is a considerable accumulation of dead wood at the executive level."

Scott Adams' *Dilbert Principle* **is a variation of the Peter Principle.**

"Promoting less productive people to higher positions prevents them from getting in the way of the small group of productive workers who get things done and keep the company going forward."

How many people in your company have been promoted beyond their abilities?

How the TED Talks Became the Ted Baxter Talks

The first TED talks brought together outstanding thinkers from T(echnology), E(ntertainment), and D(esign) to tackle difficult problems and solve them with insight and creativity.

Once intellectually stimulating presentations, TED talks have devolved into shallow performances that emphasize style over substance.

One reason this happened is that there are only a small number of really top minds, so the A-list gets exhausted and the B-listers get their chance, and so on down the line. You may have noticed this with the cast of Saturday Night Live.

Another is that TED Talks' emphasis on style became formulaic, like "reality" shows that all follow the same pattern and structure. The focus is now less on new issues and new ideas and more on high-sounding language used to impress people. Think Elmer Gantry and Oral Roberts.

The formula is simple.

- *Provide a grossly oversimplified explanation* of an issue or a problem.
- *Package astonishingly obvious observations as remarkably insightful.* For example, every person who talks about productivity will tell you how important it is for you to turn off your devices, minimize interruptions, and concentrate on the task at hand. Wow! Really?

- *Provide an easy solution*, especially of the kind that involves us buying some product or service that will do all the work for us.

Dumbing down produces, well, dumb.

TED has now been called the "insatiable kingpin of international meme laundering" and "a monstrosity that turns scientists and thinkers into low-level entertainers, like circus performers."

The New Republic says TED "is no longer a responsible curator of ideas 'worth spreading.' Instead it has become something ludicrous."

(Ted Baxter was a vain, shallow TV newsman on The Mary Tyler Moore Show.)

Which of the Seven Dwarfs is the Tallest?

This is a pointless, nit-picking question because any difference in height between the seven is too small to matter. And further, none of them are tall in any absolute sense – they're all short.

What do the Seven Dwarfs have to do with the latest Consumer Reports Automotive Reliability Ratings?

Ford's reaction to the report was to announce they were pleased to rank highest among domestic brands. What Ford didn't bother to mention was:

- U.S.-made cars occupied 11 of the 12 lowest spots.
- Every U.S.-made car finished in the bottom half.
- Asian-made cars dominated the top spots, followed by European-made cars.

Being pleased that they ranked "highest among domestic brands" is the marketing department's way of avoiding the real issue, which is that Ford's reliability ranked 18th of the 29 brands measured.

Yes, Ford ranked highest among the lowest, but the real story is that Ford is only microscopically not as bad as Buick and Lincoln.

When did *we're not last* become something to be proud of?

What else did U.S. carmakers say?

GM said it will use the magazine's survey data to "better understand our performance and where we can improve." Ford said they will review the ratings as they work to improve quality.

What, they don't have their own research?

What kinds of research are GM and Ford paying their suppliers for if they don't know about these problems until an independent organization publishes them?

USSR Finishes in Second Place in Track Meet; USA Finishes One Spot Out of Last Place.

This was a TASS headline from many years ago. Nowhere was it mentioned it was a dual meet, and the USSR and the USA were the only participants.

Was the headline *technically accurate*? Yes. Was it *deliberately misleading*? Of course.

That was the point, wasn't it?

Put on Your Thinking Caps

Six Thinking Hats is a system for conducting work sessions that claims to overcome the problems of factionalism, arguing, and groupthink.

Different ways of thinking are represented by different colored hats. Participants are directed to "put on" these figurative hats and discuss issues from that hat's particular point of view. Here is a simplified description of how it works.

The Blue Hat

The only person who wears the Blue Hat is the outsider who moderates the work session. The Blue Hat has several responsibilities:

- Outline the goals and the rules.
- Manage the agenda.
- Direct when each hat is worn.
- Formulate questions.
- Continuously drive the process forward.

White Hats

Group members put their White Hats to look at the available facts and see what they can learn from them. They are instructed to prioritize facts over opinions and beliefs and wait for all information to be presented before reaching fact-based conclusions.

Red Hats

When members wear their Red Hats, they are instructed to explore an emotional point of view, which means ignoring logic and avoiding any attempt trying to justify its feelings. Red Hats suggest solutions based upon personal feelings and hunches.

Yellow Hats

Members are instructed to be unfailingly optimistic and explore the benefits of each scenario developed. They focus on benefits, advantages, and what's good about each idea.

Black Hats

Here the task is to evaluate the solutions offered by the other hats. Black Hats are instructed to identify weaknesses, flaws, and dangers of every idea put forth by the other hats.

Green Hats

Here is where members take all the ideas, put them together, and suggest creative solutions that maximize the good and minimize the bad. They are specifically instructed to avoid the obvious.

The end product.

The Blue Hat collates all the ideas, facts, and opinions produced by the other hats and uses that information to generate an ideal solution to the problem and structure a practical plan of action.

It all sounds very good in theory, but *we wonder how well people can actually take on different personae and move seamlessly between them.*

Cool

Thomas Dorgan was an American cartoonist who died in 1929. According to his obituary in the NY Times, he introduced many slang terms into the popular culture.

Among them were some that are gone and some that lasted. When you said something was the *cat's pajamas* or the *bee's knees*, you meant it was quite special. *Dumbbell* and *for cryin' out loud* you already know.

There are many explanations for the term 23 *skidoo*.

One involves the 1901 film *What Happened on 23rd Street*. A woman steps on a subway ventilation grille that blows her floor-length skirts to knee height, greatly to her horror and "much to the amusement of the newsboys, bootblacks and passersby." A similar scene featured Marilyn Monroe in the 1955 film, *Some Like It Hot*.

***Hipster* was used in the 1940s to describe someone trendy, but the original hipsters were people who surreptitiously carried hip flasks during the prohibition era twenty years earlier.**

In the 50s, no teenager would be caught dead using any of those terms, because they had their own *rock and roll* language. *Fat City* was a great place to be. *Cool* and *boss* were used to describe anything exciting and enjoyable. On *the flip side*, the first documented use of *nerd* was in 1950 in a Dr Seuss book, *If I Ran the Zoo*.

Beatniks were bohemian types who rejected conventional society. The first one I ever saw was the fictional Maynard G. Krebs, played by Bob Denver, who some of you will know from *Gilligan's Island*. Beatniks lived in *pads*, which later became *cribs*.

The 60s gave us *mod, gear, fab* from England and from the States, *groovy, far out, bummer,* and *bogart*, used as a verb to describe a non-sharer. Surfers had their own lingo: *hodad, grungy, bitchin'*, and many more.

The 70s gave us *psyched, chill, boogie, can you dig it,* and *yo' mama*.

So when you hear a *hipster* snobbing a *nerd* for not knowing the latest *lingo*, be the wise one who recognizes some of these terms will stay with us, some will go away, and some will be recycled.

Cool.

Butch Cassidy, the Sundance Kid, and Beer

Smart businesspeople know formal research studies aren't always needed. Sometimes it's about reading signs, like the trackers in old cowboy movies. According to Butch and Sundance, Lord Baltimore was the very best at following a trail and anticipating the next move his quarry would make.

So what does that have to do with beer?

Quite a lot, actually.

The Beer Institute says beer sales have been declining in stores, restaurants, and bars for more than 20 years, hardly a passing fad.

What were some of the signs beer manufacturers missed?

Sales of wine and spirits have been steadily increasing over the same period, but Tony Ponturo, a former marketing executive at Anheuser-Busch, says "We didn't see liquor as competition" because "it wasn't beer."

Whoa, Tony!

You've got a very bad case of the *myopia of experts*, which is <u>defining your product category too narrowly</u>. This is especially prevalent among marketers siloed by product line.

Surely you remember what happened to colas?

Experts at Coke believed the competition was Pepsi (and vice-versa). This assumption was true for a while, but it ignored the growth of *category adjacencies* such as bottled waters, flavored waters, sports drinks, and more. Caught flat-footed, Coke and Pepsi ran around buying up manufacturers of non-colas.

What else were the Beer Barons ignoring?

- Big brands have been losing to small brands not only in the beverage category, but in foods, too, most obviously in the growing dissatisfaction with large mass-market brands like Kellogg's and Campbell's.
- Small-market craft beers have been putting a dent in mass-market beer sales.
- Beer sales in their most important market (men 21-27) have been declining at twice the overall rate.

So what did Big Beer do about declining sales?

- They increased prices.
- They introduced higher-priced special limited-edition beers.
- They bought up wine and liquor brands.

Haven't they made big advertising changes, too?

If you're thinking about Dilly Dilly, it's been a huge social success. The new VP of Bud Light says Dilly Dilly is responsible for "a 6 percent improvement in share of organic social media mentions."

More telling is what he did not say – there has been no increase in Bud Light sales, which we think is a much more important metric than "share of organic social media mentions."

What time is it?

WSJ quoted Heineken's Ronald den Elzen as saying "Every consumer today drinks on average one bottle of beer less a week than they did 20 years ago. If this is not a wake-up call that we have to do something, I don't know what is."

Actually it's 7,305 wake-up calls, Ron – Heineken's been hitting the snooze button for the past 20 years.

So what's next for beer? Are there growth opportunities in category adjacencies?

If we look at the category not narrowly, as beer, but broadly, as *social lubricants*, one big opportunity stands out. Several business partnerships are creating zero-alcohol, zero-calorie, cannabis drinks.

Our favorite name? Heineken Hi-Fi Hops.

7 Things You Don't Know About Wireless-only People

The Centers for Disease Control released a study that showed some things many of us would already have supposed to be true.

For the first time ever, a majority of U.S. homes are cellphone-only. A dozen years ago, nine of ten U.S. households had a landline, and now fewer than half do.

Most of us would expect the study to find the following things about wireless-only people:

- More younger than older.
- More single than married.
- More apartment renters than home owners.
- More city dwellers than suburbanites.

Given the ubiquitousness of smartphones and the replacement of analog devices by digital ones across most categories, those four findings are not surprising, but these are:

Wireless-only adults are more likely to:

- Drink heavily.
- Smoke.
- Drive without using seatbelts.
- Be uninsured.
- Have been tested for HIV.

Isn't it interesting how all five of these things share a single theme?

They all involve behaviors that lead to negative consequences (stipulating that those who get tested for HIV are likely to have engaged in unprotected sex).

Study author Stephen J Blumberg says "There is certainly something about giving up a landline that appeals to the same people who engage in risky behaviors."

Wait a minute. Why is a health organization studying wireless?

The CDC surveys many thousands of people every year. Ten years ago they were one of the first groups to realize their telephone-based surveys were missing the ever-growing segment of the population without a landline phone.

So they switched to in-person, face-to-face interviews and began including people with every type of phone configuration: landline-only, wireless-only, both land and wireless, and no service at all.

We dug even deeper into the study and found these two items, also not readily apparent.

- Hispanics are more likely to be wireless-only than Asians, blacks, and whites.
- Lower-income groups, including those living in poverty, are more like to be wireless-only than higher income groups.

Is it possible all of these things are related?

Not only possible, but likely. What we cannot infer, though, is which of these things cause the others.

Here's a risky behavior not reported in the study: The National Safety Council says cellphones cause 1.6 million car crashes a year.

No mention was made of how many crashes were caused by landlines.

TIDAL Wave

You already know music streaming is worth billions of dollars. Spotify, Apple and Pandora are big names, but did you know about TIDAL?

Owned by Jay Z, TIDAL claims that Kanye West's *The Life Of Pablo* was streamed by its customers 250 million times in just ten days and Beyoncé's *Lemonade* 306 million times in its first 15 days.

As TIDAL claims only 3 million subscribers, this raised the eyebrows of some skeptics.

The investigation began when Norwegian newspaper Dagens Næringsliv obtained a TIDAL hard drive. When they matched listening figures with subscribers, they concluded "TIDAL's listener numbers had been manipulated to the tune of several hundred million false plays."

TIDAL's data showed one subscriber played Kanye West's *The Life Of Pablo* 96 times in a single day. Another played Beyoncé's *Lemonade* 180 times within 24 hours. And so on.

When we see outlandish numbers, we like to do some simple math.

There are 1,440 minutes in a 24-hour day. *Lemonade* is 45 minutes long. Streamed continuously for 24 hours, it could be played only 32 times – not 180. At 66 minutes long, *The Life of Pablo* could be played only 22 times – not 96.

The Center for Cyber and Information Security (CCIS) is a partnership with 26 private and public members from industry, academia, and security. They forensically investigated the data and said "After thorough advanced statistical analysis we have determined that there has in fact been a manipulation of TIDAL data."

Professor Katrin Franke said *millions of users supposedly listened to a large number of tracks at exactly the same millisecond.*

"Given how targeted and comprehensive the manipulation is, it is highly improbable these distortions could be the result of a code-based bug or other anomaly," said the investigators. "There is also nothing to indicate a data breach from the outside."

The pot calls the kettle black.

TIDAL strongly denied they had manipulated streaming figures or tampered with royalty payments at the same time their legal team was attempting to shut down the study, claiming investigators falsified the data to suit their foregone conclusions.

No big deal, you say?

Billions of dollars of royalty payouts are calculated from listener figures. That is a very big deal.

The Swiss Army and Their Knife

In the late 1880s, the Swiss Army decided to purchase a new type of folding pocket knife for their soldiers. It was to be suitable for use by the army for two things other knives couldn't do: opening canned field rations and disassembling the Swiss Army rifle.

Nearly a hundred years later, it was standard issue for U.S. astronauts, who called it a small, cleverly designed, and very useful *gadget*.

The strength of the Swiss Army Knife is that it combines many functions into a small package.

It is at its most useful when you need to be able to do a lot of things in a pinch. Their standard knife includes knife blades, screwdrivers, a can opener, a bottler opener, a corkscrew, a punch, a wire-stripper, tweezers, a toothpick, a saw, a fish scaler, a ball-point pen, and so on.

The weakness of the Swiss Army Knife is that <u>it does almost none of these things well.</u>

As a result, it is rarely the first choice for any of its functions, and never for all of them.

Unless you're far from civilization, you'd never use it to open a bottle of wine or pluck your eyebrows. You'd use purpose-designed tools because they're more efficient and easier to use.

Your smartphone is a small and ingenious device that does many things, too, but it doesn't do all of them well, either.

It is fine for browsing, as a phone, and for being in constant communication. It is not the best choice for watching movies, playing games, writing, or calculating.

This is why many millions of people still buy televisions, game consoles, computers, and calculators and are likely to continue doing so for some time to come.

Big Data, Artificial Intelligence, and Cockroaches

Stephen Chen writes in The South China Post that the world's largest cockroach farm is using Big Data and Artificial Intelligence to breed 6 billion adult cockroaches a year.

The cockroaches are the raw materials of the production process for a "healing remedy" that the government says is consumed by millions in China.

The system constantly collects and analyzes humidity, temperature, food supply and consumption. It monitors genetic mutations and how these affect the growing rates of individual cockroaches.

Might there be any problems?

Zhu Chaodong, the Institute of Zoology's lead scientist in insect evolution studies at the Chinese Academy of Sciences, said it would be a catastrophe if billions of cockroaches were suddenly released into the environment, be it through human error or a natural disaster like an earthquake that damaged the building.

There are also concerns that the farm's intensive reproduction and genetic screening would accelerate the insect's evolution and produce "super-cockroaches" of abnormal size and breeding capability. Zhu said this was unlikely to happen.

What do they do with their billions of cockroaches?

When they reach the desired weight and size, the cockroaches are fed into machines and crushed to make the potion, which is said to have remarkable effects on stomach pain and other ailments. The elixir has a tea-like color, tastes "slightly sweet" and has "a slightly fishy smell", according to the product's packaging.

What's next? Raid-Ade?

When asked if ground-up cockroaches might end up in other products for humans, Subramanian Ramaswamy, a biochemist at the Institute for Stem Cell Biology and Regenerative Medicine in Bangalore, India, described the potential as fantastic. "I could see them in protein drinks," he said. Then he added,

"In principle, it should be fine, but today we have no evidence that it is actually safe for human consumption."

Deities, Ghosts, and Aliens from Other Planets

There are true believers in each category.

Those who believe in *dieties* are fragmented into hundreds of religions and sects. Each "knows" theirs is the one true way.

How many religions are there in the world today?

Most of us know the top five: Christianity, Islam, Hinduism, Buddhism, and Judaism. Each of those, of course, is fragmented into many different sects. Depending on the definition used, some say hundreds and some say thousands.

At any rate, there are many more religions than most of us know about and the probability of any one of them being the one true way is very small. The probability of more than one of them being the one true way is, of course, zero.

Those who believe in *ghosts* usually claim to have seen them for themselves, mostly in haunted houses.

Those who believe in *aliens* are divided into two groups: scientists who think it is unlikely we are the only ones in the boundless universe of trillions of stars and planets, and conspiracy theorists who think the government suppresses evidence in Area 51.

There are other creatures that belong here somewhere, such as Bigfoot and the Loch Ness monster. Each has its own true believers.

As proof, *diety-believers* use historical documents such as the Bible and the Koran as their sources. *Ghost-believers* cite mediums and seers. *Alien-believers* offer photographs and videos that are fuzzy, staged, or both.

Some believe in one, some in two, and some in all three.

It would be interesting to study the intersects between these groups. I'd especially like to know more about people who believe in all three.

How many do you believe in?

Order, Please

Most Western societies read from left to right and from top to bottom. As a result, we quite naturally assume that when it comes to lists of things, the most important ones come first.

This has a profound but often ignored effect on how we go about building lists.

Most of us try to build lists in a single step. When we do this, we are trying to do two things at once: create the list and determine the sequence.

Task switching research tells us both these things will go poorly *unless we take them one at a time*. We constantly sidetrack and slow ourselves down by bouncing back and forth between identifying the steps and determining the sequence. We struggle to figure out the sequence before we have all the parts.

Here's what works better.

Break the activity into two steps.

First, identify what we can without determining its importance or assigning it a priority. A good way to think about this two-step approach is as *the difference between nominating candidates and voting on them.*

Next, when we have plenty of nominees, we should ask ourselves:

- Is our list comprehensive?
- Are there redundancies?
- Can we combine closely related items into categories?

- Do we need to pull other items apart into smaller components?

- Are we likely to quit too soon, saying we've done enough?

- How do we push beyond the easy, the apparent, the obvious?

Then we should choose a conceptual framework.

What are some of the ways we organize lists? Alphabetical, chronological, top of mind, importance, and others. How about desired emphasis? Paid search results? You can think of more.

Another way of sorting items in a list is by law. This we see when we read labels on packaged goods in grocery stores. Here the law has decreed that ingredients must be sequenced in declining order by the amount of each present in the product. The rationale is to prevent consumers from being tricked.

The FDA and headline writers know that people always assume the item that heads a list is the most important one.

When making a list, choose your sequence carefully, as the sequence will always affect the outcome.

Take a look at the lists your company uses. What do you see?

Which Is It?

Most businesses define customer problems as unwanted headaches, obstacles, messes, and predicaments.

The exceptional ones don't.

Exceptional leaders understand problems are usually of our own making and they take responsibility for them. They see problems as opportunities to learn and improve because they:

- Understand that high customer satisfaction scores are too often artificial.
- Acknowledge customers' problems are very real and not to be ignored or dismissed.
- Commit to actively seeking and investigating problems. The more we look for problems, the more we find and the less we are likely to be taken by surprise or act too slowly.

Fast Company says "Acknowledging and learning from mistakes allows you to lead by example, and encourages your team to see mistakes not as the end of the line, but as the beginning of growth."

Challenges.

Harvard Business Review says the real definition of leadership is whether we treat problems as things to be avoided or challenges to be taken on.

When we see problems as challenges, we turn them into situations that test our abilities. The best problem-solvers know how to turn obstacles into opportunities.

Opportunities.

The biggest opportunity is in customer service. Studies show 80% of companies claim to provide superior customer service, but only 8% of their customers agree.

This enormous disconnect means *90% of all companies could benefit by providing better customer service than they do now.*

The opportunity available to all companies is to be more courteous, more efficient, and more helpful than the competition. The way to find the opportunities specific to your business is to seek out those of your customers with problems and ask them what you should be doing differently. Only a handful of exceptional companies do this.

Everyone knows problems are inevitable, so we don't expect a perfect world.

What is important is what your company does about the problems your customers are having.

Problems lead to what is an apparent paradox until you stop to think about it: *Customers who have their problems solved quickly, courteously, and professionally often become more loyal customers than those who never had a problem.*

Musical Chairs

Faced with large numbers of battlefield casualties arriving en masse, Army doctors needed to quickly determine which cases required immediate attention, which were urgent, and which could wait. This assigning of priorities and resources to one of three broad categories was called *triage*.

From its beginnings in emergency medicine, triage has been a useful way of prioritizing large numbers of anything. We can look at any set of actions and decide which need to happen first, which should go next, and which can wait until later.

For example, if we were building a house, we would construct the foundation before the walls and the roof. We would install the electrical and plumbing systems before the carpets and drapes.

Strategic imperatives.

By definition, strategic imperatives are *the essential actions that must be accomplished ahead of all other things*. Resources need to be allocated to the most critical activities and everything else needs to be aligned with them.

A marketing executive at a highly respected company once presented her staff with 27 (!) strategic imperatives. When asked by the managers which were the most important, she said they all were. This was, of course, utter nonsense.

Everyone knew 27 things could not all be the most important.

Unwilling or unable to establish priorities and assign resources, the executive had abdicated responsibility, figuratively *tossing everything on the table and saying 'have at it.'*

It was the organizational equivalent of musical chairs.

With so many "most important" things, everyone had to work on several at once and the result was <u>no one was able to devote their full attention or effort to anything</u>.

Of course, trying to align and coordinate so many things was impossible. Without definition from the leader, disagreements occurred and the staff ended up working at cross-purposes instead of cooperating. As you might imagine, this *rudderless strategy* caused a great deal of confusion, frustration, and waste.

Great grandmama would have said they were running around like chickens with their heads cut off, and she would have been right.

No one has unlimited resources.

When it comes to finite amounts of time, people, and money, executives need to determine which activities are *critical*, which are *important*, and which are *interesting*, and allocate their resources accordingly.

Pay Only for What You Keep

In 1926, the Book-of-the-Month Club started with only a few thousand subscribers. By 1951, it had sold 100 million books. The business model worked then, and it works now.

Clothing retailers have wholeheartedly embraced *the subscription model,* and why not?

- It's a regular revenue stream, not a single transaction.
- It allows customers to try on clothes before buying.
- Sellers are always looking for the next trend so they can hop on the bandwagon.

The idea is simple: we pay only for what we keep, and send back the rest.

The Upsides.

The *anticipation of getting the box and the excitement of opening it* both work on our emotions at our small child level – think of the gifts that came to us on birthdays and Christmas when we were kids.

The *surprise* factor. We don't know what will be inside the box, which appeals to our curiosity.

The *personal touch,* where style experts curate items specially for us. Psychologists say this "specialness" enhances our self-esteem.

The Downsides.

Once we have something, it's easier to keep than return. Companies know we will keep and pay for more things when they are delivered to our homes. With subscription services, we buy more clothes than we would otherwise.

Our choices are limited to picking from their choices. We do not get to choose from all manufacturers or styles. And we shouldn't be shocked to learn there are items these services want to push, which is sometimes the stuff they can't move through other outlets.

We pay more. Of course, the shipping is "free" – sorta. Actually, it's built into the price of the clothing.

And except at the very high end of subscription services, our *"personal clothing stylist"* is likely to be a low-paid cubicle worker.

Anything else?

Over time, our personalized algorithms will produce closets full of narrowed-down lookalikes. Over time, our "specially-chosen" items will be the same things everyone else "must have."

Yes, clothing subscription services are easier and can be fun – <u>when we don't mind paying more money for fewer choices.</u>

Violent Destructive Windstorms

In the United States, 1,200 tornadoes a year kill 50 people.

Texas has 149 tornadoes a year, Kansas has 93, and Oklahoma has 64. So Texas is the most dangerous place, right?

That's what most people think, but a few of us know the importance of taking more things into consideration before drawing our conclusions.

What about the state's <u>area</u>?

Texas has .0005 tornadoes per square mile. Kansas has .0011 and Oklahoma .0009, so Kansas is the most dangerous – right, Dorothy?

What about the state's <u>population</u>?

Texas has 23 million people, Kansas has 3 million, and Oklahoma, 4 million. On a per person basis, Texas has .00001 tornadoes, Kansas has .00003, and Oklahoma .00002. So it looks like Kansas again, right?

What if we define the most dangerous state as the one with the largest number of tornado fatalities?

It's Mississippi, with 10 deaths per year. This also translates to .38 deaths per tornado, which is ten times worse than Texas (.05), Kansas (.02), and Oklahoma (.04)

There are at least six lessons here, and maybe more.

- Never assume we have all the data.
- Don't be tricked by raw numbers.

- Calibrate numbers so we can compare them on equal footing.
- Dig deeper.
- Determine which statistic is most useful.
- During analysis, always remind ourselves of the original question.

We often need to look beyond short lists to find the real answers.

Marriage Causes Divorce

Newspapers provide their advertisers with lots of reader data.

My first apprentice-level research job out of grad school was with a Scripps-Howard newspaper in Memphis, Tennessee. One of my assignments was to unearth correlations without regard to causality. The goal of this research was not to learn, but to *find promotable items of interest to advertisers*. This strategy is an old one, and very successful, too.

Correlation and causality are among the most misunderstood of all research terms, and the ones most likely to be misused, especially by marketers and the media.

One is no more than some sort of undefined connection between things. The other is the more complex *cause-and-effect*.

Scientists say cause-and-effect is interpreted incorrectly more often than not. We would say people like to *jump to conclusions*.

Correlation is very popular with Big Data, where A.I. tools search for relationships. The other way to say it is *blindly groping in the dark*.

Red cars are twice as likely to be in accidents than blue cars.

The obvious conclusion for some is to buy a blue car. The questions researchers would ask first include "Is it *cars* that are in accidents, or *people driving cars*? Is it possible that people who drive red cars are more aggressive and less careful?" and others.

A friend bought a motorcycle.

His mother had read most motorcycle accidents occurred during the first six months of ownership. Unaware that those accidents were not related to the calendar (correlation), but to the new rider's inexperience (causation), her advice to him was to put it in the garage and not ride it for six months.

And don't forget, you can't get divorced without getting married first, so it is quite clear that marriage causes divorce.

The Other Levi-Strauss

Beginning in the 15th century and for the next 200 years, European explorers and traders roamed the world in search of peoples to conquer and resources to plunder.

In doing so, they came into contact with people who looked, dressed, and acted in ways they had never seen or imagined. And they believed these "savages" were <u>innately inferior in every way</u>.

The Report of the Philippine Commission, written in 1902, was one of the earliest formal ethnographies.

Its introduction said "The government is attempting to develop a new standard of relationship between the white man and the Malay. Success will depend on our understanding of these peoples."

The success the report was referring to was <u>how to make better workers out of the Malaysians</u>. For a very long time, ethnographies were written just like this –instruction manuals for how to dominate and control "inferior" peoples.

Then along came Claude Levi-Strauss.

An anthropologist, he had a different perspective. He saw colonialism as "the larger part of mankind being made subservient to the other, with millions of innocent human beings having their resources plundered while they were ruthlessly killed and thrown into bondage."

His NY Times obituary said "his revolutionary studies of what was once called 'primitive man' transformed Western understanding of the nature of cultures, customs and civilizations."

His studies transformed ethnographies, too.

What was important for the new ethnographies was the way he approached subjects. The old way, from the outside, was used to take advantage. The new way, from the inside, was objective, rational, and non-judgmental. The notion was *to understand different peoples and cultures on their own terms and not on ours.*

To anyone involved with conducting research into human behavior, this should still be the goal.

Mixed Emotions

U.S. President Ronald Reagan liked to define "mixed emotions" as the feelings a man has as he watches his mother-in-law drive over the cliff in his new Cadillac.

Another example involves how driverless vehicles will be programmed to react in emergencies. One is to act in the interests of the passengers and the other is to act for the greater good. Why is this important?

Because driverless vehicle technology will need to deal with moral and ethical dilemmas.

There are many scenarios involving undesirable alternatives. For example, when a pedestrian steps in front of a car that can't stop in time, the car's brain must make an unpleasant choice. Will it direct the car to hit the pedestrian, hit an oncoming car in the other lane, or swerve into a tree?

Vehicles will react by using pre-programmed formulas. Who will be making the decisions about how the algorithms are written?

The Trolley Problem.

There are many versions of what ethicists call this classic *thought experiment* in moral principles. Azim Shariff, director of the Culture and Morality Lab at UC Irvine, used one version in his study, *The Social Dilemma of Autonomous Vehicles*, published in Science Magazine.

He found most of us believe the vehicle's occupants should be protected at all costs – <u>when we are the occupants</u>. When others are in the car, we think <u>the vehicle should sacrifice itself and its occupants</u> to save us.

Heck yeah.

Few of us are surprised to hear that self-preservation wins, but where does this leave us? The proposition is <u>win-lose</u>, not win-win.

Who will be the ones to decide how driverless vehicles will be programmed to handle ethical dilemmas?

Will it be left to the manufacturers, who are all competing with each other? Will it be the government deciding what type of programming manufacturers will use? Or will it be some other entity?

Take a look at the MIT Media Lab website, Moral Machine, which they describe as Human Perspectives on Machine Ethics. They have put together an interactive set of a dozen lesser-of-two-evils scenarios. You are the one who decides which action the vehicle takes.

How do you think these dilemmas will ultimately be solved? It will be onboard A.I. issuing the instructions to the car, but it will be H.I. executives who make the decision.

Dear Diary

Sixty-seven years ago, Nielsen issued their first television audience ratings.

They claimed their sample represented an accurate cross-section of U.S. geographies, markets, homes, families, people, incomes, educations, ages, ethnicities, and more.

Two ways of measuring viewing.

Meters connected to the television measured when the set was on and what channel was chosen. The big problem with meters was that they measured only "on" and "off," and not who was watching, if anyone.

Having the television on does not mean we're paying attention to it or even in the same room with it. It doesn't mean we're awake, either. Who among us hasn't dozed off, left the room, made a phone call, or answered the door while the television was on?

To get richer data, panelists were given diaries and told to <u>record all television viewing by all viewers at all times</u>. Diaries were tedious and time-consuming to fill out, so they suffered from inaccurate and incomplete recording and reporting.

We don't watch like we used to.

People watch Netflix and Hulu and YouTube, not just traditional television. Fewer people watch live broadcasts. More view on-demand and on DVR. More watch on smartphones, tablets, and laptops, often away from home.

Two out of three people have devices for streaming and online viewing. *Who would suggest their habits are the same as those who sit in front of televisions?*

Advertisers care who's watching the ads, not the shows.

This is why they don't like us fast-forwarding through commercials.

AdWeek says Nielsen will quit using paper diaries in 2018 as soon as its electronic measurement systems are fully in place.

It's about time, wouldn't you say?

It's Time to Eat

Morbidly obese people are the subject of many studies.

In one interesting experiment, scientists manipulated the clocks so when they indicated 12 noon, it was really 11am. All the patients filed into the dining room, because it was time to eat.

The scientists fiddled in the other direction, so when the clocks said 12 noon, it was really 1pm. No one was looking for food at "real noon." The conclusion was simple: grossly overweight people ate by the clock.

Three meals a day.

We needed them when we were a nation of farmers. For centuries the U.S. was primarily rural and agricultural. Most of the work was physical – lifting, chopping, sawing, butchering, plowing the fields with mules. There was no electricity and no indoor plumbing. Water came from a well you dug yourself. The only heat for cooking and warming was a fireplace, and Siri and Alexa don't chop no wood.

Farmers would start with a hearty breakfast (no drive-through latte caramelita and bagel with a schmear) and burn off all the calories by lunch. They'd load up on calories again and then be hard at work all afternoon, home to a hearty dinner, and to bed early. No Twinkies, no Pringles, no Snickers.

We still eat our three meals a day, but instead of hard labor, we sit at desks. We often supplement our diets with midmorning, afternoon, and evening snacks.

So the advice is still the same. Eat less. Do more.

One doctor told us about his outpatient, who was on a special meal program. After a month, the patient had not lost any weight. The doctor asked if she had been eating her special meals like he prescribed.

"Doctor," she said, "Sometimes I'm so full after my *regular* meal I don't have any room left for my *special* meal."

Another One Bites the Dust

Yet another scientific study has been repudiated.

Research that demonstrated how to get school kids to choose apples instead of cookies by branding the fruit has been renounced by the Journal of the American Medical Association.

This comes long after the Cornell University study concluded that branding can be used to promote healthier eating. Publication of this work resulted in positive publicity for the authors, which translated into personal appearances and book sales.

Aaron Carroll, author of The Bad Food Bible, says the study was deeply flawed because research isn't as simple as most people think. Unless all the important issues are identified and addressed in advance, the work will be defective and the findings no better than useless, as was the Cornell study.

It reminded us of an investigation we did for Coconut Grove.

This crazy-quilt area on Biscayne Bay was Miami's first arts district. It was both bohemian and luxe; part Jimmy Buffett and part Miami Vice.

Coconut Grove had ultra high-end hotels and boutiques, all kinds of bars and restaurants, a lively street scene with pushcart vendors and street performers, and a very active nightlife.

We knew we could not capture all experiences and points of view with a typical approach.

To make sure every group was adequately represented, we held on-street interviews in the mornings, afternoons, evenings, late nights, and into the wee hours, seven days a week at dozens of different locations within the district.

We found art patrons had one image of Coconut Grove and nightclubbers had another, as did shoppers, restaurant goers, bar hoppers, and wandering tourists. Each had a perspective that differed from the others.

As you might imagine, study sponsors had conflicting ideas of what Coconut Grove should be.

Those businesses catering to the wealthy wanted to see the riffraff expelled, and those which catered to regular folks wanted to see the snobs banished to Bal Harbour. Our challenge was to find a way to reconcile their conflict.

We discovered the intersection of many different cultures was hugely appealing to art patrons, nightclubbers, shoppers, and all the rest.

Each needed the others to contribute to the gestalt that made The Grove attractive to so many different types.

Too little research bothers to be as thorough as this.

If we had not conducted the investigation across days and dayparts and sites as we did, we would not have compiled enough evidence to find the glue that held everything together.

When findings from rigorous, juried, scientific research are again and again found to be untrue, we can be certain that consumer research will be far less conscientious, and far more imperfect.

And we can also be assured that because proprietary research methods and samples are hidden to outsiders, no one ever knows, least of all The Boss.

About the Author

In 40 years of conducting research, David has taken a closer look at Bananas and Baseball, Laptops and Light Rail, Nurses and Nighclubs, Rodeos and Recycling, Tourism and Tractors, and hundreds more.

His investigations take from one week to one year to complete and cost from a few thousand to a few million dollars.

Along the way, David taught English for the U.S. Department of Defense in Vietnam, Sociology at Indiana University, Research at the University of Miami, and Human Behavior at the University of the West Indies.

At davidallanvan.com, he teaches decision-makers *how to avoid information traps.*

www.ingramcontent.com/pod-product-compliance
Lightning Source LLC
Chambersburg PA
CBHW030705220526
45463CB00005B/1908